FROM MY FAMILY TO YOURS

poems by

Gary Beaumier

Finishing Line Press
Georgetown, Kentucky

FROM MY FAMILY
TO YOURS

Copyright © 2019 by Gary Beaumier
ISBN 978-1-64662-033-3 First Edition
All rights reserved under International and Pan-American Copyright Conventions.
No part of this book may be reproduced in any manner whatsoever without written
permission from the publisher, except in the case of brief quotations embodied in
critical articles and reviews.

ACKNOWLEDGMENTS

To Mary, with all my love, who has been my Max Perkins in these endeavors
of mine with her keen eye for what words work. More than that, she has kept
me for the last thirty years, perhaps against her better judgement. Without her
I could do little more than write a grocery list.

And to Ben and Mara, who somehow survived my single parenting and grew
to be decent loving adults of whom I am forever proud.

You are my family.

Finally, a special thanks to Tom Kubala for the use of his exquisite and
graceful artwork on the cover of this book.

Publisher: Leah Maines
Editor: Christen Kincaid
Cover Art: Tom Kubala
Author Photo: Mary George Beaumier
Cover Design: Elizabeth Maines McCleavy

Printed in the USA on acid-free paper.
Order online: www.finishinglinepress.com
also available on amazon.com

Author inquiries and mail orders:
Finishing Line Press
P. O. Box 1626
Georgetown, Kentucky 40324
U. S. A.

Table of Contents

Night Train To Paris 1

From Certain Distances In Space I Still See My Brother 2

Ten Cents 3

The Migratory Habits of Dreams In Late Autumn 4

Night Forest 5

Your Red Hair 6

Upon The Place Beneath 7

Still Life 9

The Rio Grande 10

When We Were New 12

My Father's Wishes 13

Remembering Your Repeated Attempts At Living 15

Kept Things 17

Everything's A Gun Now 18

Colic Weather 20

Escanaba River 21

Some Still Come To Ask 22

Bone And Memory 23

Failure To Thrive 25

In The Place Just Before Sleep 26

Morning Holds Its Breath 28

The Spirit Of The Horse 29

A Father Walks His Daughter Down The Aisle And Gives
    Her Away 30

To Family And Friends 31

Hart Island 32

Wordplay With Rock 34

From My Family To Yours 35

Whistling Rachmaninov 36

Night Train to Paris

Our aged bodies
surrender to the sway
and lurch of the train
as we have passed through
the long tunnel
beneath the sea

old is a foreign country
we ride to

when we get there
we will rise to higher places
sit with gargoyles
balance on high slate roofs
as light slips through us
we sleep on park benches
dry leaves chasing around
us like wicked urchins

I will fish the river
in a floppy hat
mouthing a Gauloises
and you with a book splayed
in your lap will feed pigeons the remains
of your bread while sitting
on a soft blanket
and we will glance at each other
as only such longtime companions can with a pure knowing

later we will write postcards
from an empty bistro
—trumpet notes weave into the cool dark air—
telling the children back home
we are here now
and they will not see us again

From Certain Distances in Space I Still See My Brother

Somewhere mother holds you against her breasts in a Chicago flat
—the war winding down—
while she warms a bottle and tests the milk on the tender of her wrist;
"you are my sunshine," she sings.

Somewhere you sit in a quilted coat
upon a tricycle in front of a red house,
and later still your fastball hisses over
home plate into the strike zone.

Somewhere a man says we all derive from stars,
while a holy person declares we will live forever.

You still succor your fractious babies as you pace a midnight floor.

Only just now a distant planet watches you bend to help a student
or soften your embrace to your wife in the utter dark.

Somehow you glide out of a fifth floor hospital room into a painted
    twilight,
into streams of cars and trucks and exhaust
as your family holds your emancipated body and rides with you to the
    edge of life

and somewhere a medical student
peels back what remains of you
to learn the human clockwork.

TEN CENTS

Once
I saw a man,
whose brother
had been murdered,
sidearm a coin
into a fountain
and for years
I puzzled
over what this meant.

In the years
that followed
was the cheap prattle,
of weather speculations,
and baseball scores,
while his heartbeat kept time to some
inner dirge
that held him at a remove
and his countenance only broke open once—
as he sailed the life of his brother
on a dime
into the water.

The Migratory Habits of Dreams in Late Autumn

During the first cycle you may visit your childhood home
and they will all be there as though still alive
and there may be steaming pots
on the stove and your mother will turn to you and smile
and you will sit in a chair too big for you
while your dog settles his head in your lap

during your second cycle you dream of leaves
that have loosed themselves and drift and tumble
in quiet descent and with each you
give them the names of those who have passed
and whisper sweet prayers as your rake
gathers great drifts of them to a burn pile,
their smoky incense carried up to intersect
with a flock of birds

and in the final cycle
your breathing will slow and lengthen
as your breast heaves and settles
again ever slower and someone will read to you
as you feel the press of their weight on the bed
they will read soft words from a children's book
word by word by word
and pages will rustle like leaves
and there will be no need of anything
—all is said and done—
and you will be loosed
to rise and fall at the same time
as the earth recedes
you drift higher and are carried South
while a snow accumulates and whitens
everything below

Night Forest

Once there was a woman in the night forest
who could hear above the register of most.
She would listen to mice sing in chorus
or coyotes comfort their young
over the flash and rumble of coming weather.

There was the night when I stayed in the garden
late into the hours and you called for me
and together we watched the gods
toss stars across the sky and later
we returned to our bed and I watched you
over the vastness of our pillows
as your breathing fell into a rhythm
and you separated from me.

Have your dreams returned you to a wooded place,
dusted in moonlight, where you keen your ears
to other selves, selves beyond the register of my knowing?

Your Red Hair

I hear people often die
with the televison blaring
maybe half way through
the 10 PM news
like when you were about to be born
and the man on Channel 6
led a group through exercises
as I tried to read a biography
of Georgia O'Keeffe
and I thought
   how does this happen—this program that seems to trivialize your birth?
and I don't recall one word from
that book
but when I saw you the very first time

and the nurse told me your hair was red
I was carried on some updraft of purity
And I forgot about the man doing leg lifts
and the artist who painted
flowers so big
they could almost contain
all my joy

Upon The Place Beneath

During an intense shelling
I heard
the sergeant recite:
"The quality of mercy
is not strained.
It droppeth as a gentle rain…"
until he took a direct hit
and the pages
of Shakespeare
fluttered down like a dove
blown out of the sky

Given a half a chance
they will bayonet the
Mona Lisa,
crush her smile into
the mud and rubble—
pulverize Venus de Milo
into pebbles and dust
or machine gun
Van Gogh's quiet bedroom,
the canvas holed beyond
any recognition.

So
we obliterated their
concert halls with our aerial bombs,
pianos turned to kindling,
strings burst on cellos and violins,
woodwind and brass
mangled.

Play your Beethoven now,
barbarians!

But the cruelest thing
I ever saw was
a captured soldier's
copy of Rilke
propped against a tree
to use for target practice
each poem reduced to confetti
as he watched
his face dropping lower
and lower.

Still Life

Shall we give away our things?
Free the house of all but us?
We'll share a can of soup
and some crackers
and keep our quiet company
between spoonfuls.

We are a cubist painting in blue tint
titled "Old Couple Eats Dinner."
We are the dissonant strains of a
symphony tuning up,
the discontented dialog
of a theater production.

Once we performed such a dance,
whirring and spinning and trailing
our garments along the way.
Can the old still dance a little,
I wonder?

I read the disintegration
of your smile
after you shift your gaze
from me

but say nothing
so as not to rupture
something in our time/space
continuum.

Let me release my dark birds,
send them skyward this clear night
that gifts us all its stars,
and reach across and shelter
your free hand in mine.

The Rio Grande

After you ran
to that godforsaken
border town, son,
I took
a plane
to find you.

In a blizzard
they
de-iced the wings
again and again
as I gave in to
sleep
imagining
I could still hear the
"tock tock" of your heart
monitor
before you were born,
like footfalls down a
corridor,
predicting all the steps you'd
take in life
but
it didn't predict this.

All the while
the jet struggled
upwards,
driving snow
traded for a
harsh blue sky.

When I came upon you,
my boy,

I resisted holding
you in my arms
for a long moment,
sensing it would
give you
no comfort.
So the best I could do was
leave you broken
and coax you back home
where you might be fixed
by others who were damaged,

even though

to be broken
has a beauty
all its own
that someday
you may put
your arms around it.

When We Were New

Of late I have come to think of rivers,
like the one that flowed below ground
near the bungalow
and how, when the city busses
would rumble down Washington Boulevard,
it registered in the seismology
of the waterbed;
tributaries of movement
worked into my dreams.

Of late I have come to think of you there,
the first time
all choreographed
and mingled
and coursing
and swelling,
flowing beneath me.

And later, lain and sweated
window open, we heard
the announcer's voice
carried on the summer air
all the way from the ballpark;
you ran your finger
along the vein
in the fold of my arm
and in our stillness
the whole world pulsed,
trains thrumming,
a lazy plane overhead
as all things
commemorated in harmony
in the afterward
of our communion.

My Father's Wishes

My father,
all his days,
was tracked
by a wolf
three paces behind;
he'd warn me of this blood beast.
Then one day
late into his years
that wolf ate my father's heart.

There were days
though
when the wolf fell behind.
I knew this was so
when my father would sing the old songs
in a crooner's voice
as he readied himself
for his day.
Or in the evening
when he'd relight his cigar stub,
slick with spit,
and work through a quart of beer
that would cast an amber light
on the kitchen table.

In the summer now
I rise early to run
before the sun breaks over the water
and my father keeps pace,
working through my thoughts.
There are different sounds in this rural place—
birds call in their easy glide—
but I hear his raspy breath
overlapping mine,

and for all my days
I'm kept in the company
of a ghost and a beast.

Not far into the run
my body yields
to a slipstream of motion
outpacing the voices
and the dread
and all my self-inflicted thoughts—
if for just for a moment—

and even as he recedes from me
I see him in his dented brown fedora
cigar in his teeth
as he watches my graceful stride
and maybe he's saying,
"You keep this moment, son, as long as you can."

Remembering Your Repeated Attempts at Living

Looking back now
you should have been admired
for dodging cars in downtown traffic
wishing to be broken
against chrome and steel

...congratulated for
confessing to the cashier
at the drugstore
that you were in a
state of grievous sin
(though your transgressions
could have only been slight)...

...applauded for trying
to jump from a moving automobile,
opening the door to a press
of air and blur of pavement,
because the world spun
too fast for you

and cheered when you shuffled the halls
of the psychiatric unit
nearly insensible from thorazine...

But no one heard the
desperate eloquence
of your gestures; your attempts

Life blessed you
with its curses
and by the the time
you mouthed the shotgun
that burst your eyes from their sockets
those eyes weren't seeing much
anymore

anyway...

or maybe they were
looking toward
your next incarnation

Kept Things

Dad was a hoarder
child of the great depression
keeper of little things
non dairy creamer
pouches of sugar
secreted in pockets
tucked in the back of drawers

During his fights
with my mother
he'd reach back in his memory
and take out his
greivences
"Unfair" my mother would say
"to bring up something
that happened so long ago"

...until one day he bloodied
the kitchen with
a catsup packet he burst
on the counter
and replied to
her, "but I'm still hurt
after all these years."

Later my mother brought
him his dinner
while he hid behind
his newspaper nurturing
is wounds
and an uneasy peace would
last for several days.

Everything's a Gun Now

At the bar where he got shot
I was in the line of fire

The three year old
at the food store
holds a banana
like a pistol

"One Killed in Bar Brawl"
the headlines said
Can you be wounded and not shot,
I ask

people laugh in rapid fire
rat a tat tat

One man threatened
with a cue stick
the other
pushed a gun
into the soft of his belly

I've got the thousand yard stare until
the car with the broken muffler
sounded like a gun

He doubled over
after a mute report

a middle finger
can blow my head off

Face gone cardboard grey

It is writ holy
that
you're a militia
of one

life ebbed into a blood puddle

The double barreled guy
on the radio
turns words to bullets
Eventually I'll get what's
coming to me, he says.

Colic Weather

The wind was a bombardment of ice and snow
that morning when you returned from the barn
to say your old gelding had died of colic.

Later I winched him out of his stall
and carefully dragged him behind the tractor
to a clearing beyond the pasture.

His plush winter's coat could not conceal
the articulated bone over his once muscled flank
We had known his last days were nearing.

As you cut off a portion of his tail with
your pocket knife for a remembrance
you said to me " I never partnered better
on any horse then him.
Too bad humans aren't that easy".
You gave me a hard look
as you snapped the knife shut
and walked toward the house.

The ground yet unfrozen
yields to the back hoe and I pack
the earth down over him
so coyotes won't dig him up.

When I return to the house
you hand me tea as a peace offering
but that night I hear the yip and cry
of a pack over your restless sleep
and I worry things won't stay buried
...but then I worry things will.

Escanaba River

In dreams my father skates
the Escanaba River.
The ice hard frozen and dusted
with snow that swirls
ghostly behind him
as he flies breakneck
toward a sundown
that sets the pine and birch on fire.
He's lean in that way teens are,
with a thicket of black hair,
earflaps up, daring the cold.
Blades bite the ice as he sways
into a rhythm of greater speed
until he pivots and backward
glides in a lazy "S".

This was his glory!

There are days when
I superimpose myself in this past
—momentarily I become the lord of time,
the curator of some cataract memory—
and there he is, largely unformed,
neither husband nor father.
As I meet him this way,
our checkered
relationship and
estrangement
is yet to be.
So we walk companionably
to my grandparents
past yellow windows,
cheeks and noses red and numb
and tightened from the frozen air.

Some Still Come to Ask

I should have been a student of the sky
to watch squadrons of geese make passage
beneath low autumn clouds.
Stars could lift my heart as I hold forth with
astronomical terms like "nebula" or "quasar"
and,
while in a hammock,
held in broad trees, I'll know
branches are emissaries
to other realms,
where the moons overpower reason.

I could acquaint myself
with the retired
who fish along the quay
and see their days in total
and find their peace
in the lap and lull of the water,
speaking just to quietly ask
"Are they biting today?"

I should have studied
the nomenclature of the old
and listened to their lamentations
—bad hearts and sad memories—
just to know that some still come to ask,
"Was this not heaven?"

Bone and Memory

One of the last soldiers
of the Great War
-little more than
bone and memory-
prays to his late wife-
because his
God was a casualty
of the trenches.

He yet feels the sweep
of her hand
on his shoulders
when,
between dreams,
she checked for him
in their bed
to assure herself
that he really
returned to her

...and she settled him
from night terrors
gathering him to her body
The screams of artillery shells
And dying men

(Men hold so stoic a pose
until they shatter
completely)

His milky eyes
and damaged ears
have let his mind
mingle the past and present
so that to him
she is still beside him
while his lips move
to beseech her
with a lover's catechism.

"Give me the mercy
Of your touch
The solace of your breath
Into my breath
the caress of your voice
That I may dwell
In the safety that is you"

Finally a nurse
presses a straw to his lips
as 11:11
marches across
the face of the clock.

Soon the war will be over.

Failure to Thrive

This road is remembered
like a young river,
switchbacks and oxbows,
and your bare feet on the dash
while you nursed a Pabst,
tranced by the wood and
field whirring by,
as my battered car
swayed through another bend
and chased a sundown up one more hill
until we climbed a lookout tower
and you sat on the rail
one hundred feet up.
I should have known then
that one day you'd let yourself fall.

Now this old river runs pretty straight
and in the half light of a winter's eve
a lone doe crosses the ice.
I think she means to remind me of something,
but I'm long practiced in the art of forgetting.

In The Place Just Before Sleep

After she bequeathed you
a teapot she rode
the jet stream to a distant land.
Do you recall?

Old memories disconnect
in the upper strata
unaffected by the tug
of the planet
until they return to you
in the place just before sleep
and you free fall
back to consciousness one last time
as you catch them.

In the morning you linger
in the amniotic
wash of the shower,
aged body savaged by the exertions
of gravity,
and you wail an old ballad
against the acoustics of the tiles
as the memories cascade
until the one that
takes you back to tea.

In that pot
a steep of chamomile's vapor and
particles of the yellow flower
loosed in the warm brew
made ceremoniously and sweetened
to her liking
and then the touch
from cautious and tentative
to furious in short moments
with the bold unlayering

of wools and cottons,
surrendered to one another
by turns, and finally
her name in your head streaming
to this very moment
to your last moment
to be the last thing you will know.

Morning Holds Its Breath

Raise a glass to that which did not come to be.
Here's to arms that never held,
To lips never having kissed
wispy baby scented hair.
Take a deep drought to breasts
that remained unpurposed and
smash the crockery to bits
to this the biggest non event
of all your days.
You've kept it in the quiet too long.

And so late in our years
—our faculties diminished—
I search the house for you
on a predawn winter's morning
(a morning that holds its
breath in some portent of snow)
only to find you in the garden
—cooing to a carefully cradled emptiness—
until a flake alights on your cheek
and you drop your arms to your sides
and let yourself absorb everything.
It is then I know you've lost your place
between the longing and the real.

The Spirit of the Horse

There are deep impressions in the grass,
tracks from your truck
and muddied sod from the vet
who "put him down"
and finally
from the renderer
who took his lifeless mass away.

Once
he took flight in the pasture
throwing up clods of earth.
All that power and grace
so easily extinguished

On some morning
after the last turn
in your sleep
you may hear a
whinny or a nicker
and not know
if his spirit visits.
And all the longing
for him
divines into this unguarded
moment
or in the stillness
of a snowscape
a moon set
will throw a shadow
and that shadow
will be a horse.
And should you run
out to the new snow
and find it hoof pocked
it is all because
their living and their passing
pressed so deeply
on your mind and in your soul.

A Father Walks His Daughter Down the Aisle and Gives Her Away

Some mornings
the soft caress of sleep lingers
as his mind straddles the millennia

it is then when he sits
and burns in some pandemonium
of words and darkness
like a shot that ricochets in his head

then his thoughts alight
upon watching her
watch the world
from two and a half feet
back when she straddled his hip
and locked her sticky fingers
around his neck

and that will happen still when
she takes a lover or
swears an oath to marriage
just as his father carried him down the hall
half asleep
and he carries him still
as one moment carries another

So may she heft the violence of her words
and know how they become lodged in another
and may she curse her father
that she was not readied for this
and curse again that she was
carried too long—
or not enough—

but may the struggles with her lover
dissolve into tenderness
and may the press of his lips,
sweet upon her forehead,
gentle the last of her thoughts.

TO FAMILY and FRIENDS

This is a weak signal
from my rapidly dimming universe.
I should have seen it coming
when I couldn't remember
where
I parked the car
that day.
So this insidious creep of time
has brought me
to a loss
of purchase
on words and names
and places.

I am weightless,
untethered
my heart gunning
beat and beat and beat,
in inky panic,
any evenness
gone and
no way home

So just a final transmission
before I hollow more;
I have loved you
one and all.

Hart Island

When I was seven
I'd lie in the autumn grass
and pretend to be dead,
my hands clasped solemnly,
like when they laid out my grandfather,
inhaling the scent of burning leaves,
as light and dark danced over my face.
Family and friends wept over me
and, because I was seven,
I could hear them
and I could play with death so easily.

On a slip of an island off New York
they number the trenches
where they stack the unclaimed
three deep,
a million and counting.
Rikers inmates,
with infinite tenderness,
lower babies
who lived only short minutes
after birth.
Mothers who sign
for a city burial
never know they'll have no plot
to grieve over.

Maybe the strains of Saint Saens
will waft over this subterranean world
and reanimate
the estranged,
the anonymous,
into some ghastly carnival of dance.

Far into the night
a shard of moonlight
cuts across my pillow
to steal my sleep.
I zombie walk my old body
with blankets and flask
to the bed of our rusted pickup.
The moon playfully sails
behind a thick meringue
of clouds
as I compose myself
and surrender
to the variations of darkness
and dream of a million
untended souls.

In a rum-addled stupor
I awaken to an apparition
performing a curious dance
—until I realize it's my love
come to claim me.

"Watch the night with me
a little longer," I beg
and then ask her
if she needs a place
to grieve over
should I be the first
...but she just shakes her head
in a way I know to mean
"You crazy old man"
and kisses my cheek.

WORDPLAY WITH ROCK

There was the summer
he harvested rocks
from the beach.
Sand pumiced his feet
and the water painfully cold.

There was the day
his boy came home
after all those years
only to take a hit
and unravel everything
and all he could do was watch.

...and at season's end
he drank coffee
under unleafing trees
weighted yet spectral
with stars piercing down.

He wondered how it works with rock.
Does it crackle
when you flamethrow the butane
into the bowl?
Does the euphoria
slam into you
exactly eight seconds
after you suck it into your lungs?

After eight years
did you get back
that righteous high
or are you chasing it
still?
And will you keep chasing it
until you are under a rock?

Did you think
he didn't goddamn care?

From My Family to Yours

After my brother was killed in Iraq,
he often loomed in my thoughts
and once I even saw him on my drive home,
standing in a distant field
looking slightly
out of place.

Sometimes at 3 a.m.—when I am a casualty
Of broken sleep—I wrap myself
in his fatigue jacket, light a joint,
and stare into the emptiness of the night.

Over beers while on leave,
he told me he was ordered to fire
on a car that crashed through a checkpoint.

"I think they were
just scared,"
he said.
"The three kids
in the back seat
killed too.
The smallest
with big eyes just
staring at nothing."

After telling me this,
he said,
"Maybe I'll be their retribution."

Whistling Rachmaninov

Father of my father
our lives never overlapped
as our two hands might have
you died in a train yard
the same year as Rachmaninov
father of my father.

I secreted scraps of information about you
that fell from my parents' conversation
like confetti
father of my father.

Time's music has danced me on
father of my father
should my life share its last days
with the first of a little one
I will think on what strands of you he carries
and maybe he'll alert to the cry of a train
that will sound a note like "Vocalaise"
and I will whistle the rest as I hold him and
he quiets into sleep
and then I'll whisper
"I am the father of your father."

CPSIA information can be obtained
at www.ICGtesting.com
Printed in the USA
BVHW031425171019
561336BV00001B/19/P